# GOLD

For list of National Distributors visit
www.cwr.org.uk/distributors
Unless otherwise indicated, all Scripture
references are from the Holy Bible:
New International Version (NIV),
copyright © 1973, 1978, 1984 by the
International Bible Society.
Other version used: NKJV:
New King James Version, © 1982,
Thomas Nelson Inc.
Editing, design and production by CWR.
Printed in Croatia by Zrinski
ISBN: 978-1-85345-665-7

# GOLD

## 100 WINNING THOUGHTS

FROM THE AUTHOR OF
*GOD'S LITTLE BOOK OF CALM*
RICHARD DALY

**CWR**

# INTRODUCTION

Many athletes dream of winning a gold medal, devoting years to rigorous training, personal sacrifice and hard work. Yet there is only one gold to aspire to, and so many fall short of their lifelong ambition. Nevertheless, as encapsulated in the Olympic creed written by its modern founder, Baron Pierre de Coubertin:

*The most important thing in the Olympic Games is not to win but to take part, just as the most important thing in life is not the triumph but the struggle. The essential thing is not to have conquered but to have fought well.*

These words have many spiritual parallels. In Scripture we are called to 'run with perseverance', to 'press on towards the goal' and to 'endure' to the end. In this Christian race, there are no rank orders of positions; everyone who takes up this special race becomes a winner. There are no losers for those who are in Christ.

This little volume is designed to encourage and strengthen you in this spiritual walk. Open it at any page and be inspired.

ON YOUR MARKS
**GET SET**
**GO!**

0:00:00

# KEEP PRESSING ON

When God pushes you out of your comfort zone en route to your destiny, expect to go through some unfamiliar, anxiety-producing territory. It's the only way to go from striving to thriving.

I press on towards the goal
to win the prize for which
God has called me
heavenwards in Christ Jesus.

**PHILIPPIANS 3:14**

0:02:00

# NURTURE
## YOUR *GIFT*

**God gives talent.
Hard work transforms it
into unlimited potential.**

Every good and perfect gift
is from above ...

**JAMES 1:17**

0:03:00

# BELIEVING IS SEEING

Visualise what the reward of winning will be. Develop a mental picture of this success.
Now let this image be the fuel for your motivation.

For as he thinks in his heart, so is he.

**PROVERBS 23:7,** NKJV

# DO
## *THE THING YOU FEAR*

You gain strength, courage and confidence by doing the thing which you think you cannot do.

'Be strong and courageous. Do not be terrified; do not be discouraged, for the LORD your God will be with you wherever you go.'

**JOSHUA 1:9**

# **SEEK** *INSPIRATION*

When you're inspired to perform, you gain an extra gear that can take you to the next level of your performance; a level that you thought never existed.

'Call to me and I will answer you and tell you great and unsearchable things you do not know.'

**JEREMIAH 33:3**

# LEARN FROM YOUR ~~MISTAKES~~

Failure is an opportunity to begin again, this time more wisely.

My flesh and my heart may fail, but God is the strength of my heart ...

**PSALM 73:26**

0:07:00

# GET
# UP AGAIN

Our greatest glory is not
in never falling but in rising
again every time we fall.

... for though a righteous
man falls seven times,
he rises again ...

**PROVERBS 24:16**

# SET YOUR GOALS

If you are not sure where you are going, you'll probably end up just anywhere.

In all your ways acknowledge Him, And He shall direct your paths.

**PROVERBS 3:6,** NKJV

# THINK BIG

Seeing yourself as God wants you to be is the key to personal growth.

'The God of our fathers has chosen you to know his will ...'

**ACTS 22:14**

# *TURN DREAMS*
# **TO REALITIES**

'I say to you today, my friends, that in
spite of the difficulties and frustrations
of the moment, I still have a dream.'
(Martin L. King Jr.)
**What about you?**

We are hard pressed on every side,
but not crushed ...
struck down, but not destroyed.

**2 CORINTHIANS 4:8–9**

# BE NOT DISMAYED

Man's extremity is God's opportunity.

'With man this is impossible,
but with God all things are possible.'

**MATTHEW 19:26**

# SEIZE THE
## MOMENT

A winner is always ready for
the opportunity when it comes.

Be very careful, then, how
you live — not as unwise but
as wise, making the most
of every opportunity ...'

**EPHESIANS 5:15–16**

# LIVE THE
# *OLYMPIC* SPIRIT

The most essential thing in the Olympic Games is not the winning but the taking part; the essential thing in life is not the conquering but fighting well.

(Pierre de Coubertin – founder modern Olympics)

The race is not to the swift, or the battle to the strong ...

**ECCLESIASTES 9:11**

# CHERISH YOUR SUPPORTERS

No matter what you accomplish,
somebody will have helped you.

They confronted me in
the day of my disaster,
but the LORD was my support.

**2 SAMUEL 22:19**

0:15:00

# ENJOY
# THE MOMENT

We're so busy watching out for what is ahead of us that we don't take time to enjoy where we are.

This is the day the Lord has made; let us rejoice and be glad in it.

**PSALM 118:24**

0:16:00

# BE TRUE TO YOURSELF

Be yourself. Above all let who you are and what you believe shine through.

... whatever is true, whatever is noble, whatever is right, whatever is pure, whatever is lovely ... think about such things.

**PHILIPPIANS 4:8–9**

# LEARN TO BE
# CONTENT

We have no right to ask when problems come,
'Why did this happen to me?' unless we ask
the same question for every joy that comes our way.

... be content with what you have ...

**HEBREWS 13:5**

# DON'T WORRY,
# BE HAPPY

Being happy doesn't mean
that everything is perfect.
It means that you've decided to
look beyond the imperfections.

Happy are the people
whose God is the LORD!

**PSALM 144:15,** NKJV

JUST

0:19:00

DO
IT

Don't wait.
The time will never be just right.

Today, if you hear his voice,
do not harden your hearts ...

**HEBREWS 3:15**

# VALUE THE SUPPORT OF OTHERS

To achieve anything worthwhile,
you need people; family, friends, mentors –
you can't make it without others.

A cord of three strands is not quickly broken.

**ECCLESIASTES 4:12**

# AVØID NEGATIVE THOUGHTS

Just because you fail, that doesn't make you a failure.

No, in all these things we are more than conquerors through him who loved us.

**ROMANS 8:37**

# REBOUND

Don't add insult to injury by letting disappointment mire you in hopelessness and despair. Get back on track quickly. There's always hope for a better tomorrow.

Blessed is he whose help is the God of Jacob, whose hope is in the LORD his God.

**PSALM 146:5**

**0:23:00**

**DON'T PROCRASTINATE**

Be a self-starter.
Do it now!
Beware of the paralysis
of analysis.
Be a person of action!

See, I set before you today
life and prosperity ...

**DEUTERONOMY 30:15**

0:24:00

# SPEAK WELL OF OTHERS

**Use your words to build confidence in others.**

... encourage one another daily,
as long as it is called Today ...

**HEBREWS 3:13**

# AVOID
# LIMITATIONS

**Don't be afraid to think big.**

But when he asks,
he must believe
and not doubt ...

**JAMES 1:6**

# BE HUNGRY
## FOR SUCCESS

If you're fully focused and willing to pay the price you can get it done.

When you eat the labour of your hands,
You shall be happy, and it shall be
well with you.

**PSALM 128:2,** NKJV

# SEEK INNER
# STRENGTH

What lies behind you and what lies before you are small matters compared to what lies within you.

'And I will put my Spirit in you ...'

**EZEKIEL 36:27**

# PUT GOD F1RST

You have the greatest chance of winning when your first commitment is to a total and enthusiastic relationship with the all time, undisputed, undefeated champion of the world.

Who among the gods is like you, O LORD?

**EXODUS 15:11**

# REACH YOUR POTENTIAL

To be the best you can be in your given pursuit is all that can possibly be required of you.

... you will always be at the top, never at the bottom.

**DEUTERONOMY 28:13**

# BECOME A GEM

Your God-given talent in life is like a rough diamond. Allow Him to fashion, shape and develop it into a masterpiece of beauty.

'Like clay in the hand of the potter, so are you in my hand ...'

**JEREMIAH 18:6**

0:31:00

# VALUE YOUR EFFORTS

The secret to success is no secret ... just hard work. That's it!

But diligence is man's precious possession.

**PROVERBS 12:24,** NKJV

# DO THE RIGHT THING

You can't do the wrong thing and get the right result on your path to achieving – honesty is the best policy.

And as for you, brothers, never tire of doing what is right.

**2 THESSALONIANS 3:13**

# REMEMBER YOUR ROOTS

Share success with friends, family, teachers, co-workers, everyone who helped you get there.

Praise the LORD, O my soul, and forget not all his benefits.

**PSALM 103:2**

# FOLLOW YOUR
# INSTINCTS

To perform to your best you need to look out for opportunities and take steps based on your best instincts to act on them with all your heart.

'... your ears will hear a voice behind you, saying, 'This is the way; walk in it.'

**ISAIAH 30:21**

# USE THIS AS YOUR MOTTO

I can do everything through him
[Christ] who gives me strength

**PHILIPPIANS 4:13**

0:36:00

# VALUE YOUR EFF○RTS

When you know that you've tried your very best at any given task, be content ... all that is left for you is improvement.

I have learned the secret of being content in any and every situation ...

**PHILIPPIANS 4:12**

# KEEP A COOL HEAD

Humility in your achievement
is a wonderful virtue ...
it is the direct opposite
to being proud.

Pride goes before destruction,
a haughty spirit before a fall.

**PROVERBS 16:18**

# NO PAIN *NO GAIN*

Every reward comes with a degree of struggle. Every winner recognises that. Don't be put off by the hurdles set before you; learn how to soar over them.

Let us fix our eyes on Jesus, the author and perfecter of our faith, who for the joy set before him endured the cross ...

**HEBREWS 12:2**

# RUN TO **WIN** ||||

In the spiritual realm there are no winners or losers, first or last, highest or lowest. In the race of life all who endure to the end are victorious.

Run in such a way as to get the prize.

**1 CORINTHIANS 9:24**

# LEAVE A MEMORABLE LEGACY

**As he looked back on his life, the apostle Paul wrote ...**
'I have fought the good fight. I have finished the race, I have kept the faith. Now there is in store for me the crown of righteousness ...'

**Let this be your final testimony.**

**2 TIMOTHY 4:7–8**

# RECEIVE TO GIVE

To inspire is to be inspired. To motivate is to be motivated. You have to possess the very thing you want others to receive.

'Give, and it will be given to you.'

**LUKE 6:38**

# *PURSUE* WITH
# *CONVICTION*

In order to achieve anything of personal significance you have to obtain a total belief in what you are doing.

'We should go up and take possession of the land, for we can certainly do it.'

**NUMBERS 13:30**

0:43:00

DON'T STAY DOWN

Endurance is getting off the floor one more time than you've been knocked down.

... but those who hope in the LORD will renew their strength.

**ISAIAH 40:31**

# KEEP
## IMPROVING

Continually search for ways to keep learning, growing and developing. Always aim for the next level in your life.

But I discipline my body
and bring it into subjection ...

**1 CORINTHIANS 9:27,** NKJV

# MAKE
# SOMETHING
# HAPPEN

0:45:00

**Nothing will just fall into your lap.
You have to create opportunities.**

'So I say to you:
Ask and it will be given to you;
seek and you will find;
knock and the door will
be opened to you.'

**LUKE 11:9**

0:46:00

# FOCUS ON YOUR STRENGTHS

To be an effective winner spend more time focusing on what you do well rather than on what you do badly.

Do not neglect the gift that is in you ...

**1 TIMOTHY 4:14,** NKJV

0:47:00

# BELIEVE

There is an old saying:
'You can if you will';
make it a new motto
in your life today.

'Don't be afraid; just believe.'

**MARK 5:36**

# 0:48:00

# *MOTIVATE*
## YOURSELF

Most failures in life occur when we listen to the negative thoughts that flow into our mind. Guard against this by focusing on who you really are in Christ.

... we take captive every thought to make it obedient to Christ.

**2 CORINTHIANS 10:5**

# LOOK FOR OPEN DOORS

God always has an open door
for you in life. It's up to you
to walk through it in faith.

'See, I have placed before you an
open door that no-one can shut.'

**REVELATION 3:8**

# *THE FIRST*
# SHALL BE LAST

If you want to lead on the highest level
be willing to serve on the lowest level.

'For he who is least among you all
– he is the greatest.'

**LUKE 9:48**

# KEEP GROWING

Read six to twelve books a year in your chosen field of specialisation. Continuing to learn in the area where you are an expert prevents you from becoming unteachable.

Get wisdom, get understanding ...

**PROVERBS 4:5**

0:52:00

# BE AN OVERCOMER

The most successful athletes
are those who never let failures
and disappointments in their field
have the final word.

Endure hardship with us
like a good soldier of Christ Jesus.

**2 TIMOTHY 2:3**

# FINISH IN STYLE

It's not how you start in the Christian race,
as long as you start ... but it's how you finish.
Endure to the end!

... let us throw off everything that hinders and
the sin that so easily entangles, and let us run
with perseverance the race marked out for us.

**HEBREWS 12:1**

0:54:00

# PUT CHRIST
# *F1RST*

When you make Christ a priority in your life,
He will take care of your other priorities.

'But seek first his kingdom and his righteousness,
and all these things will be given to you as well.'

**MATTHEW 6:33**

0:55:00

# SET YOURSELF
## *FREE*

Your dream is an untapped potential.
It does not have to remain that way.
Set it free by stepping forward
in faith.

'According to your faith
will it be done to you.'

**MATTHEW 9:29**

0:56:00

# EXCEL

**God's desire is that you become the best you can be. Don't be satisfied with half-hearted efforts.**

If you fully obey the LORD your God ... The LORD will make you the head, not the tail.

**DEUTERONOMY 28:1,13**

# USE YOUR
## *SECRET WEAPON*

Use the potential that the Holy Spirit has already implanted in you. It will be your staying power.

'Not by might nor by power, but by my Spirit,' says the Lord Almighty.

**ZECHARIAH 4:6**

# STAY IN THE GAME

After you have done your best to accomplish your task today you still may not achieve it. However there is always another day. Keep trying.

Therefore I do not run like a man running aimlessly; I do not fight like a man beating the air.

**1 CORINTHIANS 9:26**

# SOAR ABOVE
# YOUR OBSTACLES

Champions are few and far between. They see beyond the challenges, risks, obstacles and hardships. In your journey in life don't focus on these mountains ... focus on the mountain mover.

'I tell you the truth, if you have faith as small as a mustard seed, you can say to this mountain, "Move ..." and it will move.'

**MATTHEW 17:20**

# A MOTTO FOR LIVING

**Citius – Altius – Fortius**
**Swifter – Higher – Stronger.**
(Pierre de Coubertin)
**Olympic Motto**

Not that I have already obtained all this,
or have already been made perfect; but I press on …

**PHILIPPIANS 3:12**

0:61:00

# TRY
# SOMETHING
## *NEW*

Go out of your way today to do
something different that will
stretch you mentally,
emotionally, physically or
spiritually. Challenges
change us for the better.

'Call to me and I will
answer you and tell you
great and unsearchable things
you do not know.'

**JEREMIAH 33:3**

0:62:00

# AVOID
## COMPLACENCY

Most people are only one idea, one thought or one moment away from their breakthrough. You never know what lies just around the corner. Keep going!

'... I will wait for my renewal to come.'

**JOB 14:14**

**0:63:00**

# CLAIM YOUR REWARD

Your life has a special purpose,
regardless of the environment
you were brought up in.
Don't let a negative past
infiltrate your positive future.

Forgetting what is behind and
straining towards what is ahead ...

**PHILIPPIANS 3:13**

0:64:00

# KEEP *GOING*

You are not finished when you are defeated.
You are finished when you stay down.

I press on towards the goal ...
**PHILIPPIANS 3:14**

**THINK**

**POSSIBLE**

0:65:00

It's what you learn from your mistakes that will define your quality of experience. Every mistake or failure has a lesson of life to make you a stronger person.

For when I am weak,
then I am strong.

**2 CORINTHIANS 12:10**

0:66:00

# POWER
## YOUR WILL

If you are determined enough
and willing to make sacrifices,
you will go far.

Teach me to do your will,
for you are my God ...

**PSALM 143:10**

# HAVE
# FAITH

**True champions put their total trust in God.**

Trust in the LORD with all your heart ...

**PROVERBS 3:5**

**AIM FOR HIGHER GLORY**

Let us not forget that while it is a good feeling to be a winner in the eyes of the world ... it will be an infinitely better feeling to know you are a winner in Christ.

'His master replied, "Well done, good and faithful servant ... Come and share your master's happiness."'

**MATTHEW 25:21**

# BECOME A
# PRODUCT OF
## THE MASTER

Before anyone else knew of your existence, God was working in secret to make you into the person He wants you to be. Be assured He is still working on you to this very day.

How precious to me
are your thoughts, O God!
How vast is the sum of them!

**PSALM 139:17**

0:70:00

# *MISSION*
# POSSIBLE

God created you with special abilities.
Your unique DNA means that only you
can accomplish what He specifically
designed you to do.

For we are God's workmanship,
created in Christ Jesus
to do good works ...

**EPHESIANS 2:10**

# DON'T LOOK BACK

Even when you can't see what God is doing ...
be assured He is working on your case –
keep running in faith.

I will instruct you and teach you
the way you should go; I will
counsel you and watch over you.

**PSALM 32:8**

# LOOK TO JESUS

Is there an area in your life where you are still questioning the outcome? Trust in God, knowing that He is always one jump ahead.

... being confident of this, that he who began a good work in you will carry it on to completion ...

**PHILIPPIANS 1:6**

# TAKE THE PLUNGE

For significant growth to take place it will mean being willing to step out of your comfort zone. Take that leap of faith today.

'See, I am doing a new thing!
Now it springs up ...'

**ISAIAH 43:19**

# LET GOD
# *PROMOTE YOU*

A great coach is someone who believes in you and teaches you to operate at your potential. There is no better person to fit that specification than the One who designed you.

'With [God] are wisdom and strength,
He has counsel and understanding.'

**JOB 12:13,** NKJV

# GIVE IT YOUR ALL

Why not make a personal commitment today to focus on doing your best and giving 100% in the task that is set before you?

Whatever your hand finds to do, do it with all your might ...

**ECCLESIASTES 9:10**

# TURN YOUR NEGATIVES
## TO POSI+IVES

Don't let failure crush and paralyse you. Use the very blocks in your path as stepping-stones that will lead you to the next level.

If I must boast, I will boast of the things that show my weakness.

**2 CORINTHIANS 11:30**

# TAKE GOD'S ADVICE

The Bible is your training manual. It contains all the instructions necessary to help you not just to finish the race, but to run in style and to be a true champion. Read it and keep it with you at all times!

All Scripture is God-breathed and is useful for ... training in righteousness ...

**2 TIMOTHY 3:16**

# EXERCISE STAYING POWER

The original Greek word for Holy Spirit is *paraclete* which means 'advocate' or 'one who comes alongside'. Be assured as you run the Christian race that you are not alone.

'Never will I leave you;
never will I forsake you.'

**HEBREWS 13:5**

# KEEP *GOING*

No matter what difficulties you are facing today, don't let them keep you down or stop you. There is no situation that God can't get you through. Wait on the Lord.

We are hard pressed on every side
... but not in despair ...

**2 CORINTHIANS 4:8–9**

0:80:00

# KNOW WHERE YOU BELONG

You don't need a gold medal or a certain high score to know you are significant. You are already significant because of who you are in Christ.

'I have summoned you by name; you are mine.'

**ISAIAH 43:1**

# BE PREPARED
## FOR FAME

Whatever accomplishments you achieve in life, people will always want to exalt you. Never forget who gave you the strength to get to where you are today.

I will remember the deeds of the LORD …

**PSALM 77:11**

# HURDLE OVER THE BARRIERS

Circumstances may wreck your plans but God is not helpless in your turmoil. He can take your calamities and turn them into a victorious blessing in disguise.

This is the victory that has overcome the world, even our faith.

**1 JOHN 5:4**

# FOLLOW THE DIVINE PLAN

0:83:00

Sometimes God takes us on a journey in life that we do not wish to go on, travelling along a road we do not wish to use, to bring us to a place we never wish to leave. God knows best.

And we know that in all things God works for the good of those who love him, who have been called according to his purpose.

**ROMANS 8:28**

0:84:00

# CHOOSE MORE THAN GOLD

Whatever you may accomplish in life, always remember that a relationship with Christ is infinitely more valuable and more precious than gold.

... your faith – of greater worth than gold ...

**1 PETER 1:7**

# DON'T RUN
## *AHEAD OF*
## *GOD*

In order to run effectively in the Christian race we also have to learn to 'Stand still, and see the salvation of the LORD' (Exod. 14:13, NKJV).

... those who wait on the LORD
Shall renew their strength ...

**ISAIAH 40:31,** NKJV

0:86:00

# KEEP HOLDING ON

Trust that God is present and working behind the scenes for you, even when you can't sense His presence.

You will show me the path of life ...

**PSALM 16:11,** NKJV

# *VALUE*
# YOUR EFFORTS

Achievement is never an accident.
It is the culmination of many years
of learning from past mistakes.

Teach us to number our days aright,
that we may gain a heart of wisdom.

**PSALM 90:12**

0:88:00

# LIVE UPRIGHTLY

God is desirous for you to succeed in life but more desirous for you to build up your character.

He has showed you, O man, what is good ...

**MICAH 6:8**

# GIVE HONOUR
## WHERE IT'S DUE

In any accomplishment remember the glory
is not about you or your strength or willpower.
It's about the One who designed you, empowers
you and gives you the drive to succeed.

He gives strength to the weary
and increases the power of the weak.

**ISAIAH 40:29**

0:90:00

# DEPEND ON GOD

God says, 'Without Me you can do nothing.'

Great is our Lord
and mighty in power;
his understanding
has no limit.

**PSALM 147:5**

# STRIVE FOR THE
## *HEAVENLY PODIUM*

To hear God Almighty say in your ear 'Well done, my good and faithful child, share my joy forever' is the best gold medal ceremony that awaits anyone who trusts in Jesus.

'This is my Son, whom I love; with him I am well pleased.'

**MATTHEW 3:17**

# *VALUE* YOUR
# SELF-WORTH

Your sense of value and personal
worth does not come from your
performance. Your true value
and worth comes from God's
love for you.

'... for whoever touches you
touches the apple of his eye ...'
**ZECHARIAH 2:8**

# RUN WITH
# CONFIDENCE

It's natural to question God during trials.
But God sees the entire picture and
always has our best interests at heart.

'I am the Alpha and the Omega,
the First and the Last, the
Beginning and the End.'

**REVELATION 22:13**

# *LEARN* FROM YOUR EXPERIENCES

Accomplishments in themselves
are not so important to God;
He is more interested in the process
and what we learn on the journey.

Blessed is the man
who finds wisdom,
the man who gains
understanding.

**PROVERBS 3:13**

# HAVE YOU GOT WHAT IT TAKES?

**The difference between try and triumph is a little 'umph'.**
(Marvin Phillips)

Never be lacking in zeal,
but keep your spiritual fervour ...

**ROMANS 12:11**

# TOMORROW CAN BE
*A BETTER DAY*

Many of life's failures occur
when people do not realise
how close they were to
success when they gave up.

'Be strong and courageous,
and do the work.'

**1 CHRONICLES 28:20**

# STICK TO THE PLAN

Persistence is doing the thing you don't really want to do but know is best for you in the long run.

My God, my strength in whom I will trust ...

**PSALM 18:2,** NKJV

0:98:00

# KEEP UP *THE PACE*

Reaching your goal is a great reward. Maintaining that achievement is where the real test begins.

'I will strengthen you
and help you ...'

**ISAIAH 41:10**

# KEEP
# HOPE
# ALIVE

0:99:00

When the world says, 'Give up',
Hope whispers, 'Try it one more time.'
(Anon)

'... I will uphold you
with my righteous right hand.'

**ISAIAH 41:10**

# TAKE ONE STEP AT A TIME

Take the first step, in faith.
You don't have to see the whole
staircase. Just take the first step.
(Dr. Martin Luther King Jr.)

Now faith is being sure of
what we hope for and certain
of what we do not see.

**HEBREWS 11:1**

Courses and seminars

Publishing and new media

Conference facilities

# Transforming lives

CWR's vision is to enable people to experience personal transformation through applying God's Word to their lives and relationships.

Our Bible-based training and resources help people around the world to:
» Grow in their walk with God
» Understand and apply Scripture to their lives
» Resource themselves and their church

- Develop pastoral care and counselling skills
- Train for leadership
- Strengthen relationships, marriage and family life

and much more.

Our insightful writers provide daily Bible-reading notes and other resources for all ages, and our experienced course designers and presenters have gained an international reputation for excellence and effectiveness.

CWR's Training and Conference Centre in Surrey, England, provides excellent facilities in an idyllic setting – ideal for both learning and spiritual refreshment.

**CWR** Applying God's Word to everyday life and relationships

CWR, Waverley Abbey House, Waverley Lane, Farnham, Surrey GU9 8EP, UK

Telephone: **+44 (0)1252 784700**
Email: **info@cwr.org.uk**
Website: **www.cwr.org.uk**

Registered Charity No 294387
Company Registration No 1990308

# Many people think the Bible is ...

# BORING*

## *But CWR daily devotionals are changing that.

Our range of daily Bible-reading notes has something for everyone – and to engage with even the most demanding members of the family!

Whether you want themed devotional writing, life-application notes, a deeper Bible study or meditations tailored to women or the growing minds of children and young people, we have just the one for you.

**To order or for more information**, including current prices, visit
**www.cwr.org.uk/store**
or a Christian bookshop.

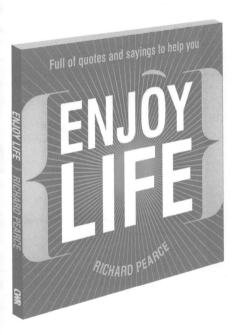

# Meet the challenge of living by faith

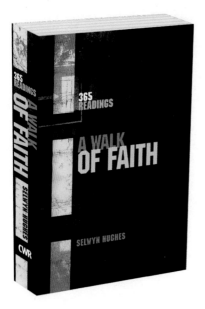

These undated, daily Bible-reading notes are specially selected to help you attain levels of courage, strength and wisdom that only God can provide.
Each of six topics covers two months, for a whole year of encouraging Bible reading, brief commentary and suggested prayers that will draw you closer to our tough and tender God.

### A Walk of Faith One Year Devotional

(Previously published as *Walk in Faith* in CWR's Pocket Devotional series)
*by Selwyn Hughes*
374-page paperback, 120x176mm
ISBN: 978-1-85345-603-9